HOME WATCH SERVICES

A Guide for Starting Your Own Home-Based Business

By George Winovich

INFINITY
PUBLISHING

Copyright © 2005 by George Winovich

ISBN 978-0-7414-2554-6

Published by:
INFIꓓITY
PUBLISHING
INFINITY PUBLISHING
1094 New DeHaven Street, Suite 100
West Conshohocken, PA 19428-2713
Info@buybooksontheweb.com
www.buybooksontheweb.com
Toll-free (877) BUY BOOK
Local Phone (610) 941-9999
Fax (610) 941-9959

Printed in the United States of America

Published October 2012

ACKNOWLEDGMENTS

This book is dedicated to my wife, Patrice, who cheered me on to write this book with her "you-can-do-it attitude."

A special thanks to Stewart C. Brown, a friend and neighbor, who often talks about starting many different kinds of businesses, this being one of them.

Another special thanks to Andre Briod, another friend and neighbor, who gave me some writing guidance and direction.

DISCLAIMER

The ideas and advice in this book are based on information currently available on this subject. The suggestions in this book are definitely <u>not</u> meant to be a substitute for business advice and guidance obtained from an attorney, accountant, insurance agent or any other applicable qualified professional. The author specifically disclaims any liability arising directly or indirectly from the use of this book.

FOREWORD

In these changing economic times, more people are searching for ideas to flex their entrepreneurial muscles. The search for startup business ideas can be a result of a number of reasons. Job loss, a desire to vacate a daily structured work environment, a desire to work for one's self, or an avenue for those already retired, to avert boredom and make extra income are among those reasons.

It was this fourth reason, coupled with the downward spiraling of the stock market, and eroding nest egg of the author, that spawned the birth of this book.

However, this book is equally adaptable to all those future business owners who, for whatever reason, are seeking an avenue to carve out their own destinies in the economic world. The fact that you have purchased this book is an indication that you have researched, are interested in, or have considered the home watch business as a possible endeavor of your own.

INTRODUCTION

"Sun, fun, rest and relaxation" sounds like the perfect, engineered lifestyle. But if you possess an active mind, such a life lacks the purpose that one derives from being productive, having a sense of accomplishment and producing capital.

After a few years of basking in the warm south Florida sun, my productive juices energized me once again. It was of little surprise to me that my initial endeavors pointed to the areas of investigations, real estate and security. I had a successful career in law enforcement and another as a licensed real estate sales associate and maintained a lifetime keen interest in real estate. Moreover, I have been the owner of several real estate properties.

The business of home watch services seemed like a perfect field to enter without a large outlay of startup capital. The market certainly was there, with a large number of seasonal owners of second homes who ventured north during the summer months. I could tailor the number of my clients and mold it all into a work schedule with great flexibility.

My interest aroused, I sought information on the Internet, libraries and bookstores to find some directive material to give me a better understanding of what such a venture would entail—some insight and food for thought, "how to material" if you will, to avoid some pitfalls inherent in this type of business. To my surprise, little such material existed, thus the transformation from home watch owner to home watch author.

The information in this guide is not intended to be a step-by-step directive. It is more of a general guide that can be expanded or reduced to adapt to the comfort level of business you hope to provide and achieve. The purpose of this guide is to get you into the operational mode and generating capital in a short time frame without looking for bits and pieces of startup information that is not readily available.

TABLE OF CONTENTS

THE MARKET

The market for clients for home watch services is virtually unlimited. The number of people owning more than one home is considerable and provides potential customers willing to pay a reasonable fee for the peace of mind that comes from employing your services. Although the home watch service visits are infrequent, they afford an alternative to leaving a property totally unchecked, and can provide subsequent peace of mind for the owner.

Years ago, people would have friends or neighbors check on their seasonal properties. However, in today's climate, people are reluctant to accept this responsibility along with the potential liability. Often, homeowners are reluctant to impose on the free time of friends or neighbors.

The seasonal resident offers the best potential for a client base, given his or her time away from a primary residence. Whether it is the northerner, aka "snowbird," heading south for the winter or transplanted "southerner" heading north to visit relatives and friends, all translate to potential clients. The movement from the mid-west to Arizona, Nevada, California or other destinations to escape the rigors of winter generates the same type of migration, only to different destinations. These often-vacated residences all represent an opportunity to provide a much-needed service, or services, to a receptive market.

Another contributing factor producing an available client base is that people are more inclined than ever to not involve newly made acquaintances in their "business." They would readily pay for the services of a reliable, insured and, if required, licensed agent to provide this function and provide a report of inspection.

Real estate agencies and real estate management companies are certainly formidable competitors for this market. However, the home watch business is an ever-increasing arena, and there is certainly room for more providers of these services when offered at a competitive price with reliable and dependable service—the components of any successful service business.

THE BUSINESS

It is prudent to mention or reiterate some basic things you should assess before starting a home watch business, or any other business. Select a business that you feel you would enjoy doing and do well. You should have some basic knowledge of the operation of household appliances, mechanics and fixtures, etc. Just the mere fact that you live in a residence gives you somewhat of a starting point, and you can expand your knowledge or limit your services from there. Probably your most effective assets will be your attention to detail, your dependability and your timeliness in reporting back to the homeowner. There are ways to increase your knowledge that can relate directly to your expertise in this area and make your services more unique and desirable than those of your competitors.

New potential business owners, particularly those with limited capital, are all basically looking for the same elements in establishing a new business. The home watch services business is certainly an attractive possibility for the budding business owner. Some of the more apparent ones, elements that can make you a success, are:

- Demand has increased for this service as a result of the increase in multiple home ownerships. The economics and customs in your area and seasonal habits of homeowners will generate the demand.

- This is a business that can be operated successfully from your home with limited overhead costs. This business, like most others, potentially has the ability to grow and expand. However, the scope of this book is limited to sole or small ownership entities. As the business grows, the decision to expand is a personal one, requiring careful examination. Such an increase in size might create the need for office space outside the home, and for additional employees and their benefits. These could well impact on the percentage of profit you came to expect prior to expansion. This will be an important decision for an owner who successfully gets up and running.

- The potential of income generated from the effort expended has a great return and can easily be done on any time schedule you wish to follow. Doing your job well and having successful clients is a great avenue for generating "word of mouth referrals" and thus greater revenues.

- This is a business that lends itself to startup with relative ease and low initial capital. That being said, it precludes the establishment of some kind of business entity, which will be discussed in more detail in a later chapter. It is relatively quick, painless and inexpensive, but it is a necessary first step to limit your personal liability exposure.

- Business cards, stationery, envelopes, flyers and brochures can be printed in small quantities at commercial outlets to limit startup costs or can even be generated on a home computer with the right software.

Other necessities for startup might include the purchase of liability insurance, a surety bond and acquiring the applicable local and state business licenses, if required, and an EIN (employer identification number) from the Internal Revenue Service, if necessary. Cell phones and digital cameras would greatly enhance the efficiency and professionalism of your operation, but are not an absolute necessity at the outset.

Most households in these times already have a home computer that could be adapted to the needs of the business. E-mail is a great saver of time and postage expense. However, even with the absence of a computer, the business could easily be conducted utilizing only a typewriter, the U.S. Postal Service and a telephone.

BUSINESS ENTITIES

If you are seriously considering going into the home watch business, or any other business, you should familiarize yourself with the type of business entity that would best suit your needs. You can seek the services of an experienced attorney or educate yourself enough to file the required documentation on your own. This information is readily available at your local library, bookstores or on the Internet.

Another excellent source for information or guidance for starting a new business is through SCORE (Service Corps of Retired Executives). This is a volunteer association of businessmen and women, who are active or retired business owners. They offer their services and guidance free of charge to anyone who wants to start a new business, or needs help in solving problems in an existing business. SCORE has chapters in cities throughout the U.S.

The major advantages and disadvantages of several types of incorporation will be listed below. The prime reason for incorporation is to provide a limitation on your liability or personal exposure, among other advantages.

Another important aspect of incorporation deals with how taxes are administered and varies in accordance with your choice of corporation type. You should further investigate the respective type of each entity and determine what benefits will best help you meet your intended business objectives.

Below are listed five basic forms of business entities that are available to business owners. Corporations are set up in your respective state in accordance with state law. The sole proprietorship, partnership, C or regular corporation, limited liability company (LLC) and "S" corporation are the most common forms of business entities. Sole proprietorships and partnerships are business entities but not corporations.

This section is not intended to be a law primer, but is intended to make you aware that there are choices and benefits to each selection. If you have acquired any personal assets, you will most likely want to help protect yourself against potential liability exposure by forming either an LLC, a regular corporation or an S corporation.

1. SOLE PROPRIETORSHIP

The major advantage of this form of ownership is its ease of operation and control. This is the simplest and least regulated form of business entity. The owner operates as a sole individual business entity. All tax benefits derived by the business actually belong to the owner or sole proprietor and are taxed at the owner's individual income tax rate. This is basically another way of saying that you are the owner of a one-person business. Most businesses start out as a sole proprietorship, but often growth dictates that the structure be changed to one of the corporate forms. There is very little government regulation with this type of organization. A business permit or license is usually required to be purchased from the county where the business will be conducted.

The major disadvantage of sole proprietorship is that the owner exposes all of his personal assets for any liability or debt that may be incurred by the business. The value of the sole proprietorship is derived chiefly from the owner. A debt or liability incurred by the business is a claim against the owner. This is probably the biggest drawback of this kind of ownership.

Another major drawback of this form of ownership is that should the owner die or become incapacitated, the value of the business is adversely affected should it become necessary to continue or dispose of the business.

2. PARTNERSHIP

The major advantage of this form of business is that the tax exposure is to the partners and not the business as an entity. The income or loss actually passes through the partnership to the individual partners, who pay taxes on any income at their own income tax rates.

This business will consist of two or more partners, and the contribution of each may consist of money or other forms of contributions such as expertise or business skills. This form of business organization is similar in some respects to the sole proprietorship in that the tax benefits are enjoyed by the partners and not the partnership. This arrangement has historically spawned more disagreements between partners over the operation of a business more than any of the other business structures. This potential problem can be greatly reduced by carefully selecting your partner(s), taking into account whether you are compatible with each. More importantly, you should have a written partnership agreement in place from the onset of the association.

The major disadvantage of this form of business is that all partners expose all their personal assets for any liability and debt that may be incurred by the partnership. Another downside is that should one of the partners die, or choose to dissolve the partnership, or goes bankrupt, the entity is adversely affected. The death of any one of the partners will usually result in termination of the partnership unless the written agreement provides for the necessary adjustments.

3. CORPORATION

The corporation, also known as the "C" or a regular corporation, is a legal entity, just like a person or a partnership. It is created by filing the Articles of Incorporation in the state or states in which the entity will conduct business. This filing, when accepted by the state, gives the corporation its legal existence and right to conduct business. The major advantage of creating a corporation is that it is composed of shareholders who are not libel for the debts of the business and thus are protected against personal liability, for what the corporation does lawfully, or for its lawful debts or losses. The corporation itself is solely responsible for debts. A shareholder's maximum exposure is the total amount of his or her investment.

Another major advantage of forming a corporation is that the business enjoys the benefit of deductions for fringe benefit payments for employees and/or shareholders. These deductions might include premiums paid for benefits such as health, life, and disability insurance, or for any other protection, which can be quite costly. If a shareholder dies, goes bankrupt, chooses to leave the business or falls ill, the corporation lives on as an entity and is unaffected, as it would be in the case of a sole proprietorship or partnership.

The major disadvantage is that the corporation is taxed as a person for tax purposes on any profit realized. If the profits are distributed to shareholders, they are again taxed as income to the recipient—basically double taxation.

4. LIMITED LIABILITY COMPANY (LLC)

The major advantage of the LLC is that it is taxed like a partnership and has the limited liability aspects of a corporation. The profits and losses pass directly to the owners, as is the case with the S corporation (below). The LLC resembles the corporation in that members who are similar in nature to shareholders own it.

The major disadvantage of the LLC is that the tax and liability benefits vary from state to state. In some states, higher incomes can be taxed on a graduated basis. This is the newest form of corporation and probably should be set up through the services of an attorney.

5. "S" CORPORATION

The major advantage of the "S" corporation is that net income is taxed only once and not twice as in the case of a C corporation. All income or tax benefits pass "through" to the individual shareholders who, in turn, account for them on their individual tax filings. This form of corporation is widely used by small businesses and can be easily set up by a business owner or attorney, who offers filings at very reasonable rates. It is similar to and has the benefits of the regular corporation, without the complexity of its establishment and maintenance.

The major disadvantage is that an "S" corporation may not get the benefit of business deductions for fringe benefits of shareholders or employees that would be applicable for a regular corporation.

In making your choice of business entity, do your homework, then form the type of business entity that best meets your needs and pocketbook and protects your personal assets from liability that may arise from operation of your business. You may also want to contact an accountant and discuss how the tax implications of each form will affect your tax exposure. You should keep in mind that you may start with one type of corporation and then decide to switch to another at a later time. But be aware that, in some cases, there are restrictions and time frames that could prevent moving from one type to another.

LICENSES, BONDS AND INSURANCE

LICENSES:

Before opening your doors for business, you should be aware that certain licenses might be required by your municipality to conduct business in the boundaries of its jurisdiction. This is usually in the form of a county business tax or occupational license. If you conduct business in a city, which is within the same county, an additional city license may be required to operate in the city as well. If your business is conducted in other counties or cities, additional licenses may be required.

There are many issues that may come into play by operating a business from your residence. You may want to explore what the requirements are in your particular locale. A big obstacle in many locales is that operating a commercial business in a residential environment is not permitted. If you are operating as an entity in which the residential address is merely a mailing address, and no business is conducted on site, you may be able to locate the business from your home. The failure to investigate the tax/license consequences beforehand and/or comply with the law is foolhardy and can be more expensive if you are found to be knowingly and willfully trying to avoid your obligations.

BONDS:

Your clients take a large step when they employ your services in their absence and grant you total access to their residence, furnishings and personal assets. A valuable sales tool in supporting this trust will be the condition that all employees in your home watch services company are bonded and covered by some sort of fidelity bond to protect against employee dishonesty. You hope that you will never need to utilize this protection, but the peace of mind afforded to you and your client is well worth the relatively inexpensive premium. Some insurance sales personnel contend that if you have adequate liability insurance coverage, you can forgo purchasing a surety bond, but agree that it is a good marketing tool and relatively inexpensive to acquire.

INSURANCE:

Most successful businesses, regardless of size, carry some form of business insurance to protect themselves in this age of litigation. If you operate a home-based business, you can get a business endorsement on your personal homeowner's insurance; however, some form of business owner's policy will better serve you. This type of insurance is specifically designed for small businesses and also is reasonably priced and well worth the cost for the related peace of mind. Most of these policies have the necessary coverage included in the basic policy; however, if a specific concern is not included, it can probably be added on at a nominal cost. Business owner's insurance policies vary from company to company as to what type of businesses they will cover and the cost per policy. You are well advised to be a diligent consumer and search for a policy that adequately meets your business needs at a reasonable price.

HOME WATCH SERVICES

The types of services offered by your company will depend on the extent of your personal participation in the business and your capabilities. You will see in a later chapter that there are additional services you can offer, beyond the core business you establish, that can easily fit into your initial business foundation.

You can start with a basic or initial service and grow at your own comfort level. Even if you do not offer a premier or more exclusive package, which is an avenue for additional revenue, your clients will request services, which may be hard to decline and still retain an established client.

Keep in mind that the residence or property that is contracted and entrusted to you is probably the single most expensive investment or asset in your client's personal portfolio. It is difficult to have a hard earned or valued investment sit idle and unattended without thinking "what if." The old axiom "out of sight, out of mind" is hard to apply when the involvement is a personal residence or investment property. Your client's monthly fee, paid to you, buys a little bit of "peace of mind" at a relatively low cost. You can offer a scale of visits, ranging from one to four times monthly and offer a sliding fee scale, in essence a discount for more frequent visits.

The basic service should include a visual inspection of both the interior and exterior of the property. Basically, the purpose of the exterior inspection is to avoid problems associated with the appearance of being unoccupied, i.e., burglary or an act that may result in possible damage to the property. A simple buildup of unsolicited newspapers and advertisements sends a signal to the seasoned canvassing burglar or the thrill-seeking, home-trashing teen. A monthly report to the owner also serves as a crosscheck that the lawn mowing or snow shoveling service may be charging and not performing their services. The type of service you offer may vary from client to client. You should have a basic package of inspection and service that you offer which meets your expertise and comfort level and inclusive enough to attract customers. For instance, the main water supply should be shut off, but you should know how to turn on the water supply to flush the toilets, run the dishwasher, run the kitchen sink disposal, and all the faucets. In situations involving multi-unit properties, your client may have the water service shut off to their unit but are exposed to water leaks of a neighbor, which may or may not be the neighbor's liability for damage to your client's property. Aside from broken water pipes and leaks, flooding and break-ins, other basic services would include checks to confirm windows and doors are locked, checks that the thermostat and humidistat settings are on the proper settings, storm damage, insect problems, and mold and mildew damage. The owner should be notified timely whenever any adverse situation is noted but particularly in situations involving the presence of insects, mold and mildew. These are situations that need to be addressed quickly, or they can manifest themselves in short order and will best be addressed by professional contractors in their respective fields.

A home inspection menu can easily be drafted on a home computer or typewriter with the services you can perform and feel comfortable with offering to your clients. This menu can be tailored into a basic service menu or an expanded premium service with a la carte service choices.

Certainly, the need, comfort and safety level provided by an alarm system is quite apparent. However, it poses a problem for the absentee homeowner when an armed alarm is tripped, whether it's an intruder or a false alarm. Because the absentee homeowner often does not have a representative to respond to tripped alarms, the alarms are often not armed and are thus useless for the period the property is not occupied. This problem has become more acute given that many local police departments are assessing fines for false alarm responses after a set number.

Offering security alarm response service allows for another avenue for increased revenue generation. However, it requires a method such as a cell phone or pager, or another method, to contact you on a 24-hour basis so that you can respond timely and deactivate the alarm or alert police authorities, if necessary.

An important element of your service is the feedback your client receives relative to your inspections. This can be in the form of a routine menu checklist, provided monthly, or the need to report an emergency. This helps build confidence in your contracted services and helps relieve stress and offers peace of mind to the absentee property owner. In today's age, many people utilize home computers and certainly e-mails and digital photographs, if required, can timely emphasize a problem. These methods offer an expeditious alternative to surface mail notification with a savings of time, stationery and postage.

OTHER SERVICES

There are countless other services that can be offered by your business; however, you have to carefully examine which of these services to offer above and beyond your basic package. You may choose to include some of these in your basic or extended services or offer these other services on an "as needed basis" and not necessarily just to the seasonal customers.

Some of these other services are time sensitive or present more challenges than your standard packages, with "your time" being the crucial or critical factor. The standard plans afford you the opportunity of being flexible to conduct your inspections during different times and days of the week of your choosing. For instance, responding to security alarms moves you from the flexible mode to a more readily available status and response mode. On the flip side, additional services may make your business stand out above your competitors and may be the catalyst for increasing your client base. Obviously, if your business is just a sideline endeavor, you can be more comfortable with limited offerings; however, if this business is your sole livelihood, additional services are a good way to expand revenues. Some of these "other services" are as follows:

FIRE & SECURITY ALARMS

More residences these days are equipped with some kind of fire or security alarm. These systems may also include smoke, carbon dioxide and motion detectors. Many of these systems are connected to a monitoring service, whose job is to dispatch local police authorities if the alarm or siren is not disengaged, and the monitoring service is satisfied that some physical response is required and some danger may be imminent. Offering to respond to these alarms means that someone in your company would have to be available 24 hours each day to respond to an alarm. This situation has become more critical because with the increase of alarm ownership, the amount of responses by local police have also increased. A large number of alarm alerts are false alarms. Many police departments have instituted a program where a designated number of false alarms are free. After that, a fine is imposed for each and every false alarm they respond to above the threshold amount.

KEYHOLDER SERVICES

Property owners who are not full-time residents often permit family and/or friends to utilize their vacation or second home when they are not there. They may also offer the property for limited rentals. Access and acquiring keys are, at times, logistical problems that can be alleviated at a cost of disbursement for key management. The keys are not disbursed without e-mail or fax authorization from the owner, and the guest or renter presents a password and identification when requesting the key. An additional safeguard would be to have a security-system guest-access code. The security guest access code can be frequently changed as an added security measure.

A basic flat fee is charged for the pickup of the key during normal business hours with possible surcharge for pickup after normal business daylight hours. If the guest or renter fails to return the key, it is the responsibility of the owner to recover the key and return it to the home watch company for availability for another guest if that is the owner's desire.

VENDOR ACCESS

This service is to give property access to vendors to perform services that are directed by the owner. The home watch service employee meets the vendor and remains on site until the work is completed and then secures the property. This service is usually charged on either an hourly or flat fee basis and can include insurance inspections, appraisals for mortgage, telephone and/or cable services, deliveries, appliance repairs or any other service that the owner wants a vendor or repair person to gain access to the property during his or her absence.

VEHICLE STARTUP SERVICE

Many seasonal owners maintain an extra vehicle on site for use during their residential stays and may prefer to have the vehicle started occasionally to keep the battery charged and have the vehicle in full operating condition. The mileage should be recorded and acknowledged by the owner to preclude any accusations of misuse. The vehicle should have a full tank of fuel to preclude any need to move the vehicle. For these services, a flat fee can be charged either with your other services or as an independent service.

WEATHER WATCHES

There are a number of services that can be included under this inclusive heading. Such perils as winter storms, tropical storms, hurricanes and other severe weather actions provide an excellent opportunity to offer prior and/or post services that are great avenues to peace of mind for absentee owners of residential properties.

Prior Actions:

These services may include, depending on the nature of the inclement weather, such projects as moving exterior furniture and other items into interior or other safe locations. Some people advocate placing outdoor furniture into in-ground swimming pools during storms. However, be cautious with this method, particularly with metal items, because doing so may result in rusting or other water damage.

More time-consuming and preventive measures would be the installation of regular or hurricane shutters, if the property is equipped with such. The simple action of taping glass windows and other glass areas is a simple and inexpensive way to possibly advert some damage. The taping action will control window glass shattering to some degree but may not necessarily prevent breakage of the glass. You should not tape glass if the glass is covered with solar film.

Post Activities:

Post activities would include reversing the activities that were put into place prior to the peril and restoring the property to the original condition. Probably the most important post action would be the assessment of property damage, if any, and providing a report and/or pictures to the property owner.

HAZARDS

In previous chapters, we touched on the benefits of a home watch service to minimize or avert the problems that were the result of burglary, vandalism and broken water pipes. Of the same magnitude, or even greater, is the damage that can result from pest infestation and the growth of mold. The keys to both situations are early detection and treatment to eradicate the problems and eliminate the source. If these situations are detected, they are best addressed by professional exterminators and mold remediation (cleanup) specialists. You are not expected to be an expert in these areas, but should be able to recognize the signs of potential problems, if visually apparent.

PESTS

From time to time, everyone will experience some form of pest infestation problems. The scope can range from ants, insects, termites and cockroaches, to mice and rats. Some of these problems are more readily detected than others; however, even if there are some subtle signs, they should be brought to the attention of the owner immediately. Regular pest treatment can help keep these problems in check. Practicing good sanitation, housekeeping and trash management are obvious maintenance efforts that will help minimize the problem and future outbreaks. Obviously, keeping entry points, such as cracks or openings around windows, doors, pipes, etc., sealed will go a long way in keeping these types of problems from starting or reoccurring.

MOLD

In recent years, we have heard much more press and news coverage about the increase of mold infestation and the costly efforts to remove it if detected. Mold has been around for years and is considered harmless in an outdoor environment. It is only when it is present indoors that it is considered harmful because the mold spores are more concentrated.

Mold is found everywhere in our environment. It is recognized that mold spores generate as a result of seeking out moist or wet areas in your home, and the fact that they are living organisms they can grow if not cleaned up. When conducting your home watch duties, you should look at potential areas such as under sink traps and drains, near refrigerators, washing machines, dishwashers, hot water heaters or any other areas where water may enter and become a mold breathing ground. You can probably see or smell large areas of mold, but small areas may not be quite apparent. The presence of the black mold film may be your first evidence of its presence.

These hazards are mentioned only to make you aware of potential greater problems, if these areas are not addressed. These problems are best left in the hands of the respective field experts because inserting yourself to mitigate these problems, in a task that you probably have little or no expertise, may only complicate the problem. Your service is to "watch and report." Getting more involved in scheduling and arranging for repairs or correcting these problems moves into a different realm which is more readily associated with property management.

HOME WATCH INSPECTION CONTRACT

The most important aspect of your business is to be sure that your clients know and understand what level of service they contracted for, and it is documented in writing and signed. Later in this chapter, a very basic sample contract of agreement will be included; however, it is recommended that you tailor an agreement of your own liking and one that you feel comfortable exercising. The required information will be basically information that pertains to the client and information that pertains to the property. This can easily be composed either on a personal computer or typewriter. It delineates what the inspection frequency will be. It is recommended that a weekly inspection is the ideal service. You can structure a price scale that favors utilizing more frequent visits. For example, you can charge $40 for one visit per month and offer two visits per month for $50.

It is imperative that you have all possible contact numbers (beepers, cell phones, faxes, etc) for your client so contact can be made timely, in the event of an emergency. You will need a mailing address and/or an e-mail address to forward any necessary hard copies and/or pictures to illustrate and document a situation, should a problem arise. It is also advisable to request that an alternate contact, who will know the whereabouts of the client, be listed in the event that you are unable to reach the client.

The property information should include the full address, security alarm entry code with password, the settings for all mechanics, such as air conditioning, humidistat and furnace, and the location of all utility service panels. The client may prefer to issue you a vendor entry alarm code. The names of all utility companies, with both contact and emergency telephone numbers, that service the property, should be supplied to timely contact the utility if an emergency occurs.

ABC HOME WATCH SERVICES CO.
(Sample Contract of Agreement)

ABC Home Watch Services Co.   Page 1 of 3
123 Adams Street
Naples, Florida 12345   Date_____

Name/Client_____

Address_____

City/State/Zip Code_____

Telephone Number_____

Other Contact Numbers (Cell etc.)_____

E-mail Address_____

Address to Forward Inspection Report by Surface Mail

     Street_____

     City/State/Zip Code_____

Alternate Person Contact

     Name_____

     Telephone_____

The Standard Services Package on Page 2 will be conducted on the frequency indicated below, and agreed to, and initialed by the client.

Inspections: One Visit per month $40.00____ (Initials)

                Two Visits per month $50.00____ (Initials)

                Three Visits per month $55.00____ (Initials)

                Four Visits per month $60.00____ (Initials)

ABC Home Watch will conduct the services listed below under our Standard Services Package on a frequency of ____visits(s) per month.

STANDARD SERVICES PACKAGE

1. Exterior and interior security inspection of premises.

2. Check settings of thermostat/humidistat.

3. Run water in kitchen sink and disposal.

4. Flush all toilets.

5. Run dishwasher once per month through rinse and hold cycle.

6. Check electrical circuit breakers.

7. Check premises for water leaks or water damage.

8. Check for signs of pest infestation, mold and mildew.

9. Check refrigerator.

10. Run faucets.

Other requested services not included in the Standard Services Package will be conducted at an additional fee for services as indicated below.

1. Service _____

   Frequency of Service _____ Fee _____

2. Service _____

   Frequency of Service _____ Fee _____

3. Service _____

   Frequency of Service _____ Fee _____

25

PROPERTY INFORMATION

Security Alarm Code and Password _____

Security Alarm Monitoring Company _____

Thermostat/Humidistat Settings _____

Utilities/Location of control panels and shutoffs:

Gas _____

Electric _____

Water _____

Furnace _____

Air Conditioner _____

Security System _____

Other _____

Utilities/Name, phone #s and emergency phone #s:

Gas _____

Electric _____

Water _____

Other _____

Inspection report(s), excluding emergencies, will be forwarded once per month, encompassing all the respective month's activities.

I have read and understand the terms of this contract and have indicated such by affixing my signature of agreement below.

Client_____ Date_____

Vendor_____ Date_____

You should be aware that the author, who is a layman and not an attorney, prepared the sample contract included in this chapter. I have seen contracts that are much simpler and some that are more detailed with "legalese" language and considerably longer in length. You may feel more comfortable having an attorney review whatever contract you decide to use in the course of your business or have him draft one that he feels better suits you needs.

In the world of contracts, there are only four elements or essentials that are needed to make the contract a valid instrument. A brief synopsis of these essentials is as follows:

- Contractual Capacity of the Parties. Not all people are capable of entry into a valid contract. Factors such as intoxication, insanity, minor's status and mental competence are some aspects that may impact on whether a contract is valid or not.

- Offer and Acceptance. There must have been a meeting of the minds between the parties, with one party making an offer and the other party accepting the terms. A contract is made when all four essentials are included, and the parties have signed the agreement.

- Legality of Object. The contract must have a lawful purpose and not be enforce contrary to law or public policy.

- Consideration. In the case of your business, whatever is given in exchange in payment for your services.

These, in essence, are the four essentials of a valid contract in brief. There is more information regarding each essential readily available; however, for this purpose, I think you will understand the basic essentials of a valid contract.

The contract can be relatively brief or can contain more detailed language. It can also include, in detail, such areas as fees, payment policy, termination, status of parties, insurance, confidentiality or any other number of aspects that you and/or your attorney feel is necessary to safely protect your interests. If these four essentials are present in your contract, you have all the requirements to make the contract legally sufficient to be enforceable. The contract will be more readily enforceable if the terms are in writing and signed by the parties involved versus an oral agreement.

HOME SECURITY SAFETY TIPS

A short security briefing with your client prior to their departure will go a long way in safeguarding the home entrusted to your watch. Some of these precautions, if implemented, are not only beneficial when the property is unoccupied, but will directly add to the safety of the owners when in residence.

Start by looking at the property at a distance and assess areas that are vulnerable by such obstructions as overgrown shrubbery or other obstacles. Simply cutting back shrubbery may enhance visibility from the street view and eliminate a hiding place for a would-be burglar and add some security. Any outdoor furniture and artwork, or other outdoor valuable, are readily susceptible to theft if left in plain view.

Outdoor lighting can help neutralize some of the negatives of shrubbery or layout obstruction and may just be enough of a deterrent for a would-be burglar to select another target.

After entering a residence, the obvious checks to make sure windows and doors are secured are good places to start. There are added security measures that are available such as drilling the frames of the windows and doors and inserting removable metal pins to make these entry portals more difficult to breech. Dead bolts on the doors are another consideration. Placing a wooden dowel or metal rod in the track of a glass sliding door offers additional protection, but does not preclude the lifting of the whole door and pulling outward to gain entry. These additional safeguards are nice to have, but if not so equipped, you can only make recommendations and consequently deal with what is available and hope for the best.

Many garage doors are equipped with additional sliding track locks to secure the door; however, care must be taken to not have a mental lapse and forget to release the latches prior to opening the door. Failure to release the latches may cause damage to the door. If the garage door contains windows, they should be obscured in some manner to avoid someone making an assessment of your garage property or looking for the presence of a vehicle.

If the client is friendly with his neighbors, they may offer extra sets of eyes for recognizing something unusual occurring at the property and can notify the authorities. The neighbors should be advised by the owner that your home watch service will periodically be at the residence, and you should not be misconstrued as an intruder. Hopefully the marking on your vehicle, which can be as simple as a magnetic attachable plastic sign, will preclude this from happening. The owner may also want to advise his local police station that the residence will be unoccupied during certain dates and that your home watch service will check on the status from time to time.

Probably the most effective present day tool to safeguard a property is a home alarm security system that is monitored 24 hours per day by a security service provider. No matter how secure you can prepare your home from intruders, no residence is totally secure. It is anticipated that the collective use of all these methods, and any additional safeguards, will give the intruder the opinion that the residence is currently occupied. He may then decide that he would be better served choosing another potential unoccupied target.

These are only a handful of security safeguards available, and many other more subtle tips or recommendations are available in free police pamphlets or are available in security books at your local library or bookstore. These stated precautions would give the client the opinion that the safeguarding of his property is also your concern. Whether he adopts or employs any of your recommendations, however, is another story. At least you made the attempt, and you may be pleasantly surprised if some of your recommendations are utilized.

DEPARTURE CHECKLIST

When your clients are focused on the preparation for departing on their vacation or extended trip, they may easily overlook the necessary steps to insure the safety of the premises after their departure. This checklist can serve as a physical systematic pre-departure review to check off the areas of concern. This list can be expanded or reduced to your liking; however, it will help assure the premises are secure and safe until your first scheduled home watch visit commences. Some areas of concern should encompass some or all of the listed items.

1. Take necessary steps to stop mail and newspaper deliveries.

2. Shut off the main water supply if accessible.

3. Remove any outside furniture or other items of value and place them indoors.

4. Check that all windows and doors are properly secured.

5. Unplug computers, electronics or any other electric plugs that will not be necessary during the absence. If you have a computer modem, be sure to unplug the telephone line from the jack.

6. Set the thermostat and humidistat to recommended professional settings.

7. Hot water heater maintenance. There is a difference of opinion related to how the hot water heater should be serviced. Some professionals advocate shutting off the gas or electric power source to the heater and

draining the water. Others recommend just turning the water heater circuit breaker to the off position. Still others caution about completely shutting off a water heater because the expansions and contractions due to major temperature changes may cause damage when the water heater is turned on at a later time. These advocates recommend instead to set the water heater temperature dial to the vacation setting. The setting is more readily observed on a gas-fired water heater than an electric water heater. On the electric heater, it requires removing an access panel to observe the settings. Consult the owner's manual or someone knowledgeable with water heaters if you are unsure of how to adjust the settings.

8. Set lights and timers.

9. Prop open the doors on the washing machine, clothes dryer and dishwasher.

10. Leave the refrigerator on, but remove all food from the refrigerator and freezer. A box of baking soda may be a good idea to insure a fresh smell.

11. Shut off the water supply to washing machine.

12. Change the air conditioner/furnace filter and have the unit serviced prior to departure.

13. Have a whole house electric service surge protector installed.

14. If the property is located in a gated community, the entry gate should be properly notified to insure that the home watch services company representative is able to gain entry to the community grounds.

15. Be sure to lock your door upon departure.

These are some of the more readily exercised preparations that homeowners can take prior to departure. These actions will go a long way in reducing the odds that some unforeseen occurrence will transpire during their absence. The more preparations and safeguards that are practiced, the greater the likelihood that the period of your stewardship will be uneventful.

MARKETING

Once you have decided to start your own home watch services business, you should also begin your own marketing campaign. Advertising is expensive so you have to allocate your marketing costs wisely and gauge the results of each method.

An obvious beginning point with no cost is simply advising your relatives, friends and neighbors of your intention to start your business, and any potential client referrals from them would be greatly appreciated.

Your initial printed material will probably consist of business cards and some kind of 8½-inch X 11-inch paper printed on both sides. This sheet can be folded to generate a six-panel brochure, which can then fit into a size-10 envelope and be mailed. You may want to use a lighter weight paper for mailings and a heavier weight paper for use in sales presentations.

You can utilize many free venues to display your business cards such as community bulletin boards in supermarkets and other stores, housing plan centers and many other free display boards. These are more readily available than you may think, and now that you have an interest, you will be more cognizant of their existence. My dentist, for instance, offers a board for his patients to post their business cards in appreciation for their business.

You can select an area to target or "farm" with your brochure mailings. Try to determine what areas have large numbers of seasonal homeowners and concentrate on mailing to that area, a minimum of three times. You can determine how large an area you can afford to market.

Beyond these basic and least costly methods, you have to assess where to proceed from there. A good starting point is advertising in housing plan community monthly newsletters, if they accept outside advertising. The costs are usually rather reasonable and often are discounted if you sign up for more than one month.

Local community monthly newspapers or area journals are also reasonably priced advertising venues with which you may be able to stretch your advertising dollars. Daily newspapers and magazines are good advertising vehicles with a vast audience but are rather expensive tools.

Advertising card "packs" are mailings sent to households in "farm" areas that include cards on a number of different businesses in that area. Check these out and determine if they meet your budget.

You should obviously consider the use of a Web site. This avenue can reach a much-expanded audience; however, the cost is considerable, with no assurance of proportional customer return. The cost will depend on your computer expertise and if you can build the site yourself or need to hire a computer expert to do the necessary construction.

Once you start receiving feedback and inquiries, be sure to ask or have the ability to track how your potential customers learned of your business and continue to use that marketing tool or even expand on it if it's productive.

Once you get up and running and have clients that are content with your service, be sure to ask them to refer you to acquaintances that also need your type of service. A display folder containing letters from satisfied clients is also a good sales presentation tool.

These suggestions are just some very basic beginning steps that you may use to get up and running on a minimum advertising budget. As your business becomes more established and grows, you can reassess your marketing expenditures and make the necessary adjustments. As in other areas of your business, you will learn what works and what is not successful and can then make the required adjustments along the way.

CUSTOMER SERVICE

Now that we have gone through the mechanics of the business, there is another aspect of the operation that needs mentioning. I would be remiss if I did not include some comments regarding this topic. Customer service is as old as the business entity itself, and not much has changed over the years. One thing that has changed, however, is the expectations of customers. Customer service is directly proportional to the success of your business.

Every customer is different and will have different expectations of what constitutes superior service. Although no two customers are the same, research has indicated that there are six service characteristics that customers value more than other service elements. These service elements are as follows:

- "Now" Answers. Customers want an answer when they have a question, and they want it timely or in many cases, right away. Society has become more impatient as people's lives have become busier.

- Reliability. Customers value reliability and consistency. They expect the same or a better level of service in dealing with a vendor.

- Honesty. Customers prefer the truth, even if it is not the answer they want to hear. Do not make any idle promises if you cannot deliver the goods.

- High Quality. Customers expect a high level quality of service. If you fail to meet their expectations, they will take their business elsewhere.

- Choice of Options. Customers want to be able to choose from various options. People have access to more information than ever before, and they want to use this information to choose among alternatives.

- Special Treatment Consideration. Everyone thinks they deserve better treatment than everyone else. Customers focus on their own needs, and as a result, they are basically self-centered.

If you keep these elements in mind when dealing with customers and are successful in delivering this service, you stand a better than average chance of operating and growing your business. It has also been determined that while price is an issue, there is a differential range that does not matter to customers if they are provided with service and convenience.

The satisfied customer is probably the best avenue for generating new business. A satisfied customer will readily refer or mention the name of your business to friends, neighbors or associates, who may be in need of your type of business services. Conversely, a customer that is unhappy and is not satisfied with your service is not a good advertisement for your services.

You will encounter some customers who will not be satisfied no matter how high the level of your service. If you make a concerted effort to accommodate a customer, and he turns out to be nearly impossible to work with, you should strongly consider terminating the relationship. Firing a customer may seem unthinkable for a small or startup business, but in the long run, it is probably the best thing to do.

Life is too short to suffer and be disgruntled, so in this type of situation, it may be best for you, your employees and other customers, if you eliminate or resign the account. The "divorce" so to speak has to be done carefully and diplomatically, so you and your company are not "bad mouthed" to would-be customers. It is not easy to dismiss a source of revenue, but you have to keep the long range and best interests of your company in mind, as well as your own welfare, when making this decision.

If you exercise and conduct your business in a manner to meet these expected service elements, you should be successful and even grow your business. You will encounter bumps in the road, but if you can honestly assess your performance and are confident that your service meets the highest level, you will grow and prosper. Keep in mind that you are directing your operation and owe it to yourself to not only be successful, but in the process, be happy as well.

"WAR STORIES"

Throughout most of this book, the emphasis has been weighted on the side of prevention of damage with limited reference to the "horror stories" that can occur if properties go unchecked. Although these stories are basically cause and effect situations, they also hold some other valuable information which may be of use to either you and/or your client should you encounter such a disaster.

I was personally involved in the first story because it concerned my father-in-law, Earl, after the death of his wife, Kitty, and prior to his diagnosis of dementia and/or Alzheimer's disease.

Earl was born and raised in rural West Virginia and had a love for the sea. After a stint in the U.S. Navy during World War II, he was later employed as a ferry captain for Hatteras Yachts. Earl settled down near the south New Jersey shore and held several positions in local marinas. I mention Earl's background only to point out that it is of prime importance to keep boats well sealed and maintained to prevent leakage. Earl took this aspect to heart with utmost importance. While working days at the marina, Earl's dream was to build his own house on a lot ideally situated to take advantage of the New Jersey summer breezes and be protected, as much as possible, against the winter winds. And that he did. Working days at the marina and evenings and weekends on his house, Earl worked himself almost to a state of exhaustion until he completed his labor of love. Earl built a log cabin kit home, which I guess you can say was "hermetically" sealed. Earl was a jack-of-all-trades kind of a guy, having some "abilities" better than others, but in his mind, there was no project that he could not figure out and complete better than most. One of his "abilities" was his wielding of a caulking gun. Earl caulked every crack, nook and cranny in sight. This even extended to caulking the space between the stove and adjoining countertops, wall electrical outlet plates, etc. This caulked, tight house had little "mildew" problems when Earl and Kitty were in good health because it was open and ventilated enough not to cause any problems.

After Kitty's death, Earl lived alone with their two Maltese dogs, Cruiser and Dolly, and kept the house closed tight. It was not until Earl's hospitalization for a gall bladder operation that I traveled to New Jersey to be on site for his recovery. I had planned to stay at the house and tend to a number of outstanding issues, while Earl recuperated.

Upon arriving at the house, I opened the front door and just stood there in a state of bewilderment. The entire interior was covered with mildew. I mean not one single surface of that house had been spared. Obviously, staying there was entirely out of the question. Subsequently, it would take days to wash down every surface and every item in the interior of that house and ventilate it sufficiently to make it habitable. It was full days of labor to rid that place of mildew. It was later determined that some construction decisions contributed to the mildew problem, but being closed tight with no ventilation was another major contributor.

The sad part of this story is that on the day Earl was to be released from the hospital, he fell out of a chair and fractured his hip. That injury along with a medical diagnosis of dementia and/or Alzheimer's disease rendered him unable to occupy that house again, although he would have some brief visits before being transferred to a nursing home until his death.

If Earl was not felled by illness, he certainly would have died knowing his labor of love was put up for sale because he truly gave a part of himself to build their home.

The second story involves a mold situation that was encountered by a couple we know named Jimmy and Chrissy. The beginning was funny, but the final results were not that amusing. Jimmy found a lot of humor in the situation, but Chrissy did not see the humor in it at all. They are a fun couple who live in Florida and enjoy a good time. Jimmy loves to be the center of attention and readily admits, "it's all about me." A carefree type of a guy, Jimmy is truly engrossed in the game of golf and its gamesmanship, so consequently it consumes his free time. Chrissy conversely is health conscious and subscribes to a wide range of holistic orientations. I should add that Jimmy also has an interest in NASCAR racing.

A few years ago, after a long day on the links, Jimmy returned home, and Chrissy was away doing something else. Jimmy's sunglasses were smeared with suntan lotion, and he decided to put them in the sink with running water to clean them up a bit as he lay on the sofa to watch a rerun of NASCAR's Dale Earnhardt "hitting the wall." Whether it was fatigue, too much sun or some other factor, Jimmy was soon fast asleep, missed Earnhardt's miscue, and the water continued to run. And run it did. Jimmy awoke sometime later only to find the sink overflowing and a major water disaster in progress.

Sometime later, Chrissy, who was previously in good health and health conscious, started to encounter health problems, which she attributed to mold infestation. This would require that they vacate the premises of their home for almost one year while the repairs were made and the mold cleaned up. After they moved to their temporary lodging, Chrissy started to receive some relief from her mold-related ailments after being in a "clean" environment. I have to mention that their homeowner's coverage to cover mold-related issues was a major battleground with their insurance carrier. Fortunately, they were successful. The homeowner's insurance mold coverage in Florida, and other states, has changed since this incident occurred. Some insurers have since excluded coverage for mold entirely, while others offer minimum amounts with options to purchase more coverage as an add-on endorsement.

The purpose of this example is to make a point of insurance awareness, and that mold growth can, and does, arise and spreads quickly. A review of your homeowner's policy is a prudent task, and you may be well served to educate yourself as to your policy's mold coverage and make changes if you desire. Mold remediation (mold cleanup) is an expensive cleanup process and often requires a long time period away from the premises to complete the task.

The third story relates to a condo water damage situation that was incurred by my neighbors, Stewart and Barbara, who previously owned a nearby condo prior to moving into our Florida neighborhood. The name "Stewart" may sound familiar, and it should be, because it is the same person listed in the acknowledgement section in this book.

Stewart and Barbara are avid RV travelers and from time to time were away on RV and other traveling junkets. After returning from one of these trips, they could not believe the damage they incurred from leaking pipes from their upstairs neighbor. They would later be more surprised to learn that, in Florida, the liability for this type of damage is not the responsibility of their neighbor but would have to be a claim against their own homeowner's coverage or paid from their personal funds.

The purpose of citing this example is that although the coverage in Florida is interpreted in this manner, it differs from state to state. In some states, the same scenario would be the liability of the upstairs neighbor.

The last story was told to a real estate class I was attending in Florida. The class instructor stated that her son and daughter-in-law resided in an apartment in Kentucky. Prior to retiring for the night, which happened to be a few days before Christmas, the couple threw a load of laundry in the washing machine and went to sleep. After falling asleep, the washing machine apparently malfunctioned and started to spill water all over the floor. This continued until the water started to affect the apartment below. After being awakened by the sound of running water, the downstairs neighbors pounded on the couple's door to alert them about the problem, to no avail. In desperation, they summoned the police. The living room ceiling below subsequently collapsed and destroyed most of the contents of the room, along with the Christmas tree and gifts. The police, after also being unsuccessful in awakening the sleeping couple, assumed the apartment was unoccupied and broke down the door and shut off the water. Needless to say, the couple awoke; however, not until the damage was done.

The sad part of this story is that the downstairs neighbors were displaced from their apartment a few days before Christmas, and for several weeks after, while the apartment was repaired. The bright light was that it was later determined that the washing machine malfunctioned, and the manufacturer stood behind the product and covered all costs of repairing the damage.

The lessons learned from this story are twofold. One, leaving an appliance operating while you are out or asleep is not a good practice. Had the malfunction occurred while the couple was awake, the resultant damage may have been greatly reduced. Secondly, look beyond the damage to the source. In this case, someone had the insight to look into the source, the malfunctioning washing machine, to find another source of liability coverage. The manufacturer of the washing machine acknowledged that the machine had, in fact, been defective, which resulted in the malfunction, and agreed to reimburse the parties for all costs incurred.

These "war stories" have been cited here to raise the awareness of what quite possibly can happen if the necessary preparations and coverage are not taken prior to and after vacating a property. The other purposes are to cast some light on the insurance liability and coverage issues, sources of damage and the operation of appliances while you are out or asleep.

All precautions and safeguards go a long way in making a possible loss less likely, but if incurred, proper insurance coverage makes the incident less monetarily traumatic.

CONCLUSION

I hope that by reading this book you have answered many of your questions about starting a home watch services business and have considered it as one of your possible entrepreneurial endeavors. If you have previously re-searched this subject, I think you will agree that finding information dealing with starting a home watch services business, as a home-based business, was virtually non-existent. I believe that this publication has more information available on this subject in one volume than any other on the market.

Most of the available home or startup business books available do not include the home watch services business at all, and the ones that do contain only a page or two of general data. Whether you are already familiar with this type of business, or a neophyte searching for a business to start, you should learn something from this book.

Anyone with an average amount of learning ability and common sense can follow this primer and, in a short period of time, have a viable business up and running and generating income. This guide, if it does not contain enough data to your liking, will also point you in the direction to find the additional information you seek to meet your needs.

NOTES

NOTES

NOTES

ORDER FORM

For additional copies of this book, please send
check or money order payable to:

WINGATE PRESS INC.
P.O. Box 112469
Naples, FL 34108-0143

Price per copy is $9.95 plus $4.00 shipping &
handling or $13.95 total funds per copy.

Yes, I want _____ copies of
*Home Watch Services: A Guide for Starting Your
Own Home-Based Business*
at $13.95 each.

My check or money order for $ _____ is enclosed.

Name _____

Address _____

City _____ State _____ Zip _____

Also available on the Internet at
www.buybooksontheweb.com
or by telephone 877-BUY-BOOK (toll free)
or 610-941-9999.
Fax orders to 610-941-9959.

Made in the USA
Monee, IL
07 July 2026

56551271R00036